CONTENTS

WHAT IS THE HEART?

Your heart is about the same size as your fist.

Your heart is one of the strongest **muscles** you have. It beats about 70 times a minute to pump blood all around your body.

Even when you're relaxing in front of the TV or snoring away in your sleep, your heart doesn't take a rest. It keeps on beating, day and night, without you even having to think about it.

ACTUAL SIZE!

HEART-SHAPED

The hearts you see on Valentine's cards are based on a real heart's colour and shape. Your heart is mostly dark red in colour. It's wide at the top and pointy at the bottom, and it is made up of two halves.

In one day, your heart beats 100,000 times. In an average lifetime, it beats more than 2 billion times!

BRILLIANT BLOOD

Blood does a very important job - it carries food and water to all your body parts. It also carries another very important thing - **oxygen**. This is a gas from the air that your body needs in order to work. Each of the **cells** in your body needs a constant supply of oxygen, food and water. If the heart stopped pumping blood to your cells, they would stop working - and so would your whole body.

Your blood is constantly on the move. It can complete a journey around the body in 20 seconds. It passes through the heart twice for each journey.

Hospitals keep blood in bags. They use it to replace the blood patients lose during an operation or in an accident.

Your heroic heart beats away near the middle of your chest. If you listen closely to a friend's heart, you can hear it hard at work - making a flapping, thumping noise that sounds a bit like 'lub-DUB, lub-DUB, lub-DUB!'

BLOOD AND BREATHING SYSTEMS

Nose

Mouth

Trachea

Lung

Heart

Blood vessels

Your heart is the central part of the **circulatory system** – a group of body parts that keep blood circulating, or going around, inside your body.

The circulatory system also includes the blood vessels – the tubes that your blood flows along.

IMAGINE THIS...

Imagine taking all the blood vessels out of your body and stretching them out in a long line. How far would they stretch? The answer is about 100,000 km – or 2.5 times around the Earth!

The circulatory system works closely with another system – the **respiratory system**. The lungs are the central part of the respiratory system. Their job is to breathe in air, take the useful oxygen out of it, and put it into your blood. Air enters your lungs through tubes called airways. These are your mouth, nose and **trachea**, or windpipe. The airways are also part of the respiratory system.

Ribs

The two lungs are the dark areas on this chest X-ray. The white area in between the lungs is the heart.

Why is the heart on the left?

It's just the way we've developed. Most people's hearts are slightly on the left side of their body. This means their left lung is slightly smaller than their right lung, as the heart takes up some of the space. However, about one in 10,000 people have their heart and other organs the opposite way round. They often don't even realize until they go for an X-ray.

HEART PARTS

The heart's job is to pump blood around the body. It is split into two halves, like two pumps working side by side.

The right half of the heart pumps blood to the lungs. The left half pumps blood to the rest of the body. Each half is split into two sections, called chambers: an atrium and a ventricle.

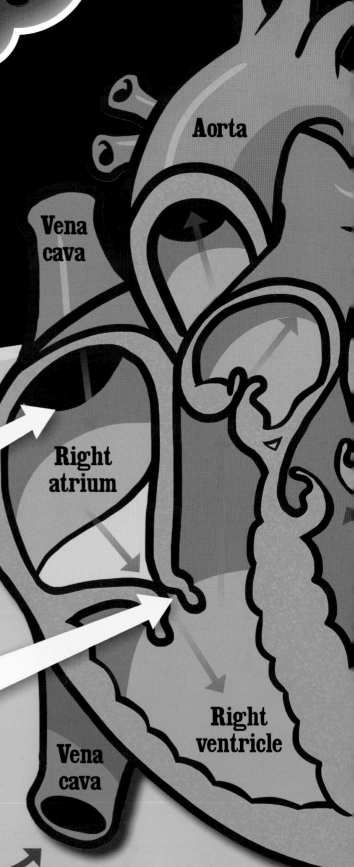

Aorta

Vena cava

Right atrium

Right ventricle

Vena cava

1. Blood coming from the body flows through the **vena cava** into the right atrium.

2. Blood passes from the right atrium into the right ventricle. The right ventricle then pumps the blood out of the heart through the pulmonary **artery**, which carries it to the lungs.

Blood always flows from the atriums to the ventricles, and never the other way.

Pulmonary artery

Left atrium

AROUND THE BODY

Blood from the rest of the body flows into the right side of the heart. From there, it is pumped to the lungs, where it picks up oxygen and drops off waste, such as **carbon dioxide**. From the lungs, the blood flows into the left side of the heart, which pumps it back around the body. As the blood flows around the body, it drops off oxygen and **nutrients** and picks up waste. Blood without oxygen in it is shown here by blue arrows.

Pulmonary veins

3. Blood coming back from the lungs flows through the pulmonary **veins** into the left atrium.

Left ventricle

4. Blood passes from the left atrium into the left ventricle. The left ventricle then pumps the blood out of the heart through the **aorta**, which carries it to the rest of the body.

Stay healthy!

The heart has its own blood supply, which it needs to keep it beating. If fat builds up in the heart's blood vessels, this can block the blood supply and cause a **heart attack**. You can reduce the chances of a heart attack by exercising and eating plenty of fresh fruit and vegetables.

PUMPING MACHINE

So you know that your heart pumps – but what is a pump? It's a machine that moves liquids or gases from one place to another.

Pumps can work in several ways, and the heart is one of the simplest types. It works by squeezing in and out. Make a fist, clench it tight, then relax it. This is what your heart looks like as it pumps.

SQUE-EE-EEZE!

The heart is made of muscle. There are muscles all over your body, and they all work by **contracting** then relaxing again. When the muscle around a heart chamber contracts, it squeezes the chamber and forces blood out of it. When the muscle relaxes, the chamber opens up and fresh blood flows in.

Atrium

Atrium

Ventricle

Ventricle

Valve open

1. The heart relaxes and fills with blood, then the atriums squeeze to push blood into the ventricles.

ATRIUMS SQUEEZE

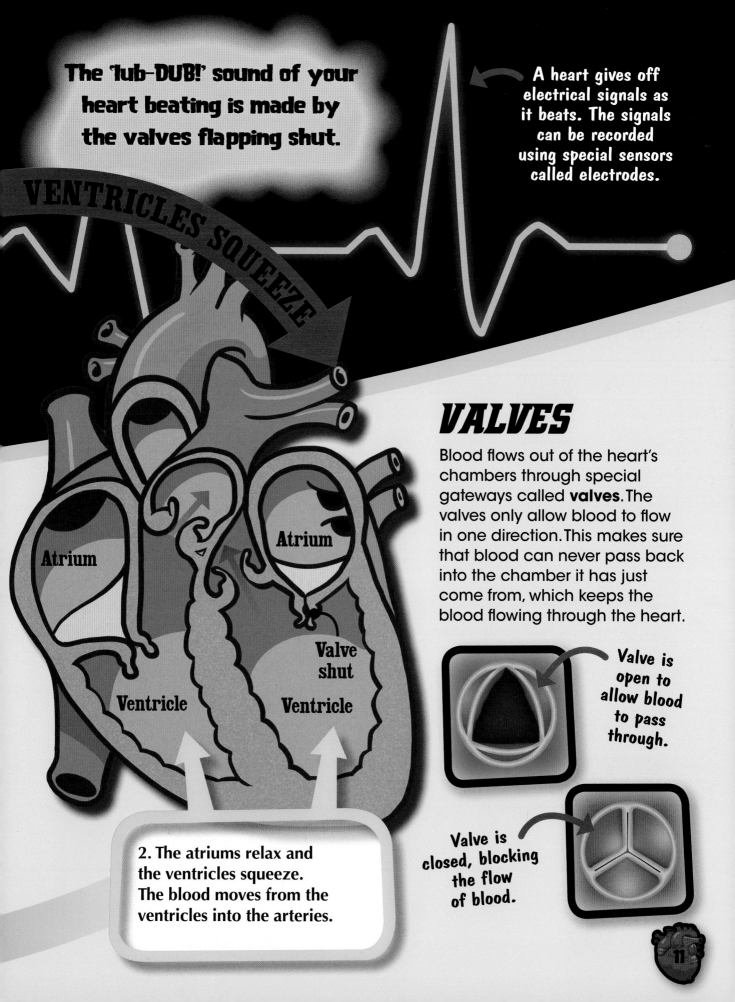

The 'lub-DUB!' sound of your heart beating is made by the valves flapping shut.

A heart gives off electrical signals as it beats. The signals can be recorded using special sensors called electrodes.

VENTRICLES SQUEEZE

Atrium

Atrium

Valve shut

Ventricle

Ventricle

VALVES

Blood flows out of the heart's chambers through special gateways called **valves**. The valves only allow blood to flow in one direction. This makes sure that blood can never pass back into the chamber it has just come from, which keeps the blood flowing through the heart.

Valve is open to allow blood to pass through.

Valve is closed, blocking the flow of blood.

2. The atriums relax and the ventricles squeeze. The blood moves from the ventricles into the arteries.

BEATING VALVES

MODEL VALVE

This simple model shows you how a heart valve works. It even makes a 'lub-dub' beating noise.

YOU WILL NEED:

- Paper cup or yoghurt pot
- Scissors
- Paper
- Sticky tape

1 Cut a hole in the base of the cup, about 1 cm across.

2 Fit the cup tightly over your mouth and breathe in and out through it. Air passes through the hole in both directions.

3 Now cut out a square of paper about 2 cm across. Put it over the hole, and tape it in place on one side.

4 Now try breathing in and out through the cup again. What happens?

What happened?

You've made a working valve. When air goes through it one way, it pushes the valve open. Air coming back the other way makes the valve flap shut. You can breathe out through the hole, but the valve stops you from breathing in.

STETHOSCOPE

Doctors use stethoscopes to hear the sounds of the heart more clearly. Use this working model to listen to your friends' heartbeats.

YOU WILL NEED:

- Cardboard tube from the inside of kitchen roll, foil or wrapping paper
- Small funnel
- Sticky tape

1 Fit the funnel inside one end of the tube.

2 Hold the funnel in place and wrap sticky tape around the join.

3 To use the stethoscope, place the funnel against someone's chest. Put your ear to the other end of the tube. Can you hear their heartbeat clearly?

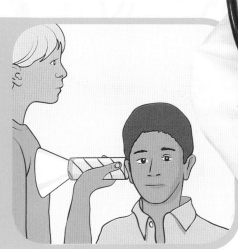

Doctors use stethoscopes with two earpieces and a flexible tube.

SPONGY LUNGS

Your lungs are two big, stretchy, spongy bags that take up most of your chest. When you breathe in, they fill up with air and get bigger. When you breathe out, they get smaller.

You can't feel your lungs as they are protected by the bones of your ribcage. But if you take a few deep breaths in front of a mirror, you can see your chest getting bigger and smaller.

What do lungs do?

Lungs suck in air from outside your body so that you can get the oxygen you need. However, only one fifth of the air on our planet is oxygen. The rest is made up of other gases that we don't need. Your lungs filter out the oxygen and pass it into your blood, leaving the other gases behind for you to breathe back out.

Bronchi

Bronchioles

Oxygen
21%

Other gases including Argon (0.9%) and Carbon dioxide (0.03%)

The air we breathe

Nitrogen
78%

Alveoli

Lung

Nose

OXYGEN IN!

When you breathe in, air enters your body through your nose or mouth.

Mouth

1. The mouth and nose take in air, warm it and catch dust and germs.

WASTE OUT!

When your cells use up oxygen, they make a waste gas called carbon dioxide. The blood carries carbon dioxide back to the lungs and it is breathed out.

2. The trachea carries air to the two bronchi, which lead to the lungs.

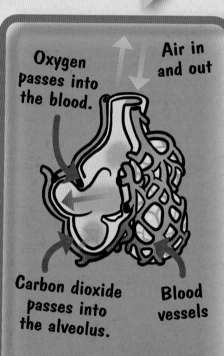

Trachea

Oxygen passes into the blood.

Air in and out

Carbon dioxide passes into the alveolus.

Blood vessels

3. From the bronchi, air rushes into thousands of tiny tubes, or bronchioles, inside the lungs.

4. At the ends of the bronchioles are tiny round air sacs called alveoli. This is where oxygen enters the blood.

Lung

When an alveolus (plural alveoli) is full of air, oxygen passes through its walls into the blood vessels around it. Carbon dioxide passes from the blood vessels into the alveolus.

15

TEST YOUR LUNG POWER

This experiment lets you measure how much air your lungs can hold in one breath. You might need another person to hold the bottle while you breathe into it.

YOU WILL NEED:

- Large, empty plastic bottle
- Washing-up bowl or bucket
- Water
- Measuring jug
- Permanent marker pen
- Bendy straw

1 Measure 200 ml of water in the measuring jug. Pour it into the bottle. Using the marker pen, mark the water level on the side of the bottle. Keep adding the same amount and marking the water level and amount on the side until the bottle is full to the brim.

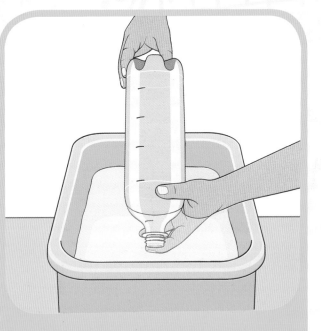

2 Half-fill the bowl or bucket with water. Put your finger over the top of the bottle. Keeping the water inside the bottle, turn it upside down and place it in the bowl. When the neck of the bottle is below the water level, you can safely remove your finger.

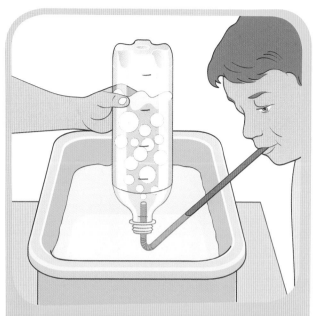

3 Bend the straw and stick the bendy end inside the neck of the bottle. Now take the biggest breath you can. Blow slowly into the straw until you can't blow any more.

4 The air from your lungs will start to fill up the bottle and push the water out. The markings show the volume of air in the bottle. This is how much air your lungs can hold, also called your lung capacity.

Can I increase my lung capacity?

Yes! You can't make your lungs bigger, but with practice you can get better at breathing in deeply and taking in more air. People who do a lot of sports or play a wind instrument such as the trumpet often have a very big lung capacity.

BREATHING IN AND OUT

Like your heart, your lungs keep on working all day and all night. You keep breathing even when you're not thinking about it.

However, if you want to, you can take an extra-deep breath, breathe in a deliberate pattern or even hold your breath for a bit. So how do we breathe?

BREATHING IN

Intercostal muscles

Rib

Flexible cartilage

Lung

Diaphragm

Ribcage gets bigger as you breathe in.

Diaphragm contracts and pulls down.

BREATHING MUSCLES

When you take a big breath, it feels as if your lungs are simply taking in air by themselves. In fact, it is not your lungs that do the work, but special muscles in your chest and stomach.

Rubbery sheet

The main breathing muscle is called the diaphragm. It is a sheet of rubbery muscle that lies underneath your lungs. When the diaphragm contracts, it pulls downwards, opening up the lungs and sucking in air. The diaphragm relaxes as you breathe out. This allows it to move up as the lungs empty.

18

Ribcage gets smaller as you breathe out.

You breathe in and out about 20,000 times every day!

RISING RIBCAGE

Your lungs are surrounded by a set of stick-shaped rib bones. These make up the ribcage. The ribs have muscles between them, called intercostal muscles. As you breathe in, one set of intercostal muscles pulls to lift the ribcage up and out, opening up the lungs. As you breathe out, another set of muscles pulls the ribcage down and squishes the lungs, pushing air out.

BREATHING OUT

Diaphragm relaxes and moves up.

HICCUP!

Hiccups happen when you eat or drink too fast, eat spicy food or laugh a lot. This causes the diaphragm to spasm, or tighten suddenly, and you suck air in very quickly. Your throat closes to stop the air, and this is what makes the 'hic' sound.

BALLOON LUNG

This experiment shows how your diaphragm helps to open up your lungs and suck in air.

1 Dangle one of the balloons inside the bottle. Stretch the balloon opening over the neck of the bottle.

2 Carefully cut off the bottom off the bottle using the scissors. Cut the neck off the other balloon and stretch the balloon over the bottom of the bottle. Secure it in place with the elastic band.

DEEP BREATH!

The longest someone has ever held their breath for was more than 20 minutes, but that's not normal! Most of us can manage only a minute or two. You have to keep breathing, or your cells will start to run out of oxygen.

Free divers try to dive as deep as they can in one breath. They can hold their breath for five minutes or more.

3 Now hold the bottle in one hand. With the other hand, pinch the lower balloon in the middle and gently pull it downwards. Watch what happens to the balloon at the top!

What's happening?

The balloon at the top is the model lung, and the balloon at the bottom is working like the diaphragm. As it pulls down, it increases volume and reduces pressure inside the bottle. This sucks air into the balloon 'lung'.

WHAT IS BLOOD?

Plasma

Blood is a liquid that carries oxygen and food around your body to wherever they are needed. Blood has other jobs, too – it fights germs, repairs wounds and helps to spread heat around your body.

You have two main types of blood cell: red blood cells and white blood cells (see page 24).

WHAT IS IN BLOOD?

Just over half of your blood is made of a thin, yellowish liquid called plasma. The plasma helps blood slide along inside the blood vessels. It also carries important things to your cells, such as dissolved nutrients and medicines, and waste that needs to be taken out of the body. In addition, it contains **hormones**, which give the body instructions, such as to make the heart beat faster.

Floating in the plasma are several kinds of blood cells.

MAKING BLOOD

Blood cells are made in your bone marrow, in the middle of your bones. The marrow releases the cells into the bloodstream. Plasma is made from the water and food you take in when you drink and eat. It passes into the blood through the intestines, or guts.

White blood cell

Red blood cell

Platelet

One tiny drop of blood the size of a pinhead contains:

5 million red blood cells
7000 white blood cells
300,000 platelets

What are platelets?

Platelets are pieces of broken-up cells. Their job is to repair cuts and damage to blood vessels. If you have a cut on your skin, platelets gather in the cut and stick together to make a **clot** that stops the bleeding. The clot combines with plasma and a stringy substance called fibrin to form a scab.

RED AND WHITE BLOOD CELLS

Most of the cells in your blood are either red or white blood cells. Red blood cells carry oxygen all around your body. White blood cells fight germs, and travel directly to the places they are needed.

A type of white blood cell called a macrophage eats harmful bacteria.

RED BLOOD CELLS

Red blood cells have a doughnut-like shape. This makes it easier for them to flow through even the tiniest blood vessels. They carry oxygen around the body and release it through the sides of the blood vessels into cells. Red blood cells also take in waste carbon dioxide. Then they go back to the lungs to pick up more oxygen and release the carbon dioxide.

Tiny blood vessels carry red blood cells past all the body's other cells.

24

WHITE BLOOD CELLS

White blood cells are bigger than red blood cells, and there are far fewer of them. There are several types of white blood cell, but they all do the same job: fighting diseases. They track down harmful germs, and try to kill them. Some do this by releasing germ-zapping chemicals. Others, such as macrophages, wrap themselves around the germs and swallow them up.

FIGHTING INFECTION

When germs get into your body through a cut, white blood cells attack the germs straight away. Extra blood flows to the area, carrying more white cells with it. The increased blood flow causes the infected area to swell up.

This climber is breathing oxygen from a tank on his back.

MOUNTAIN AIR

In high mountain areas, the air is less dense than it is at sea level. This means that there is less oxygen to breathe. Mountaineers sometimes need to carry oxygen tanks with them to help them breathe.

At the top of Mount Everest, there is just one third as much air as there is at sea level.

MEASURE YOUR PULSE

You can feel your heartbeat all around your body. Each pump of the heart makes blood surge, or pulse, through the blood vessels. Find out how to feel your pulse, and how to see it in action!

TAKE YOUR PULSE

1 Hold one hand with your palm facing upwards. Now place the first two fingers of your other hand on your wrist. Place them on the same side as your thumb, just below the crease between the wrist and the hand.

2 When you find the right place, you should feel the pulse as a little bumping sensation under the skin. To measure your pulse, use a clock or a stopwatch to count how many beats there are in one minute. This is your pulse rate.

3 Try measuring your pulse rate when you're relaxed, then again after doing some exercise, such as running on the spot for a minute. Is there much difference?

PULSE TWITCHER

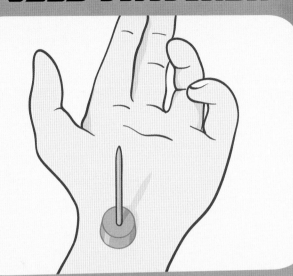

YOU WILL NEED:

- Marshmallow
- Cocktail stick

Stick the cocktail stick into the marshmallow. Press the marshmallow onto your pulse point with the stick pointing upwards. Once you get the placing just right, your pulse should make the stick twitch back and forth. Now you can see your pulse!

Exercise, such as swimming, makes your heart beat faster. This causes the blood to flow faster, so it can deliver more oxygen, and your cells can work harder. Being scared can make your heart race, too. Your body is getting ready in case you have to run away!

An average adult's pulse rate when at rest is about 70 beats per minute. Children's hearts usually beat a little faster than this.

27

BLOOD VESSELS

Arteries
carry blood away
from the heart.

Heart

The pattern of blood vessels around your body is incredibly detailed. It is a network of linked tubes with millions of branches.

There are two main types of blood vessel: arteries and veins. Arteries have thick, strong walls as they carry blood away from the heart at high pressure. Veins carry blood towards the heart at lower pressure, and have thinner walls.

BLUE AND RED BLOOD

In diagrams like this one, arteries are mostly shown as red and veins as blue. Blood leaving the heart to be delivered around the body is carrying lots of oxygen, and this makes it bright red. When blood has dropped off its oxygen, it has a darker colour. It's not actually blue, but veins can look bluish when you look at them through skin.

Veins
carry blood
towards
the heart.

Artery

LOOP THE LOOP

Vein

Blood vessels work in a loop system. Blood leaving the heart flows along large, main arteries, then branches off into smaller ones called arterioles. As they reach the cells where the oxygen is needed, the arterioles branch off into tiny capillaries. The blood flows out of the capillaries into small veins, called venules, on into bigger veins, and back to the heart.

Arteriole

Venule

Oxygen leaves the blood as it passes through the capillaries.

Capillaries

LEAKY LYMPH

When blood flows through capillaries, plasma leaves the blood vessels to deliver food and other chemicals to the cells. Most of the plasma then soaks back into the blood, but some escapes as a liquid called lymph. It flows into another network of tubes called the lymphatic system, which carries it back to the heart to be recycled.

Lymph ducts
carry lymph
to the heart.

MAKE FAKE BLOOD

Fake blood is very useful in the theatre, film and TV, where actors use it to pretend they've been injured. It's also great fun for Halloween parties!

1 Mix all the ingredients together in a bowl, stir well and – ta-daa! – realistic-looking fake blood. This blood is edible too, though you might not want to drink too much of it.

2 Make your own blood bag by putting some fake blood into small re-sealable bags and adding white sticky labels. For a vampire costume, stick a straw into one and have a drink!

Blood suckers!

Vampire bats feed on other animals' blood. They prefer cows and horses, but sometimes slurp on humans! They give their sleeping victims a painless bite and lap up the blood with their tongues.

GLOSSARY

AORTA
A large artery leading out of the heart.

ARTERY
A blood vessel that carries blood away from the heart.

CARBON DIOXIDE
A gas that is released by the body's cells as a waste product.

CARTILAGE
Flexible, bendy substance that is found at the end of bones. The ribcage contains cartilage, which allows it to expand.

CELLS
Tiny building blocks that make up the human body and other living things.

CLOT
A lump of hardened blood.

CIRCULATORY SYSTEM
The heart, blood and blood vessels.

CONTRACT
To shrink and get smaller or shorter.

HEART ATTACK
Damage to the heart muscle caused by a blockage in a blood vessel.

HORMONES
Chemicals carried in the blood that make changes happen in the body.

MUSCLES
Parts of the body that contract to squeeze or pull other body parts.

NUTRIENTS
Chemicals found in food that are useful to the body.

OXYGEN
A gas found in the air that animals need to breathe in.

RESPIRATORY SYSTEM
The airways and lungs that take oxygen into the body.

TRACHEA
Tube in the throat that carries air from the mouth to the lungs.

VEIN
A blood vessel that carries blood towards the heart.

VALVE
A one-way opening that flaps shut to stop a fluid from going back the way it came.

VENA CAVA
A large vein leading into the heart.

INDEX